EMDR

DISCOVER FREEDOM and

PEACE from learning to

process your past

By TJ Addams

EXTRAS

Disclaimer: I am not a medical professional. I am someone who has suffered through many different unsettling life experiences, quite a few different counselors and countless therapy sessions to try and manage the experiences, without much success, until now. I finally found the one that made the most significant difference in my life.

TRIGGER WARNING: The content on these pages describes the unsettling life experiences I have had. These include child and young adult maltreatment on a physical and emotional level, without limitation. Please be watchful of this and exercise caution as necessary.

DEDICATION

I would like to send a very heartfelt thank you to my awesome counselor, Laurel. I am without the words necessary to express my thanks for your hard work and patience. WE DID IT!

Also, thank you to Colleen, Lea and Maria for reading over my work and providing excellent feedback. Your hard work is most appreciated.

Finally, I want to thank the love of my life. I know it has been almost unbearable at times Thank you for being here through my anger, emotions, failures and successes. I love you!

INTRODUCTION

Some readers will not believe that a ball going back and forth on a screen or some other stimulation that causes your eyes to move back and forth rapidly can help you completely eliminate the effects of past trauma (from here on, referred to as unsettling life experiences because trauma can be a trigger word, especially if it appears here repeatedly.) But, if you are unfamiliar with EMDR, I suspect you think this guy is full of it.

According to (What is EMDR?, n.d.), EMDR (Eye Movement Desensitization and Reprocessing) is a psychotherapy that enables people to heal from the symptoms and emotional distress that are the result of disturbing life experiences. And according to (Shapiro, 1989), EMDR is "rhythmic saccadic eye movements while holding in mind the most salient aspect of a traumatic memory."

In other words, according to Booth LPC, (2021):

the memory is reprocessed, removing the unhelpful response (e.g., intense anger or quick startle) that was initially created by the intense emotional arousal. The intention is to assist a person in reprocessing a trauma so the brain is no longer reacting as if it is still in danger. When we experience high levels of distressing emotion, our logical brain "goes offline" and all of our energy goes toward the emotional brain.

Hi! My name is TJ Addams. The following pages are written by me and are from my experience with my counselor Laurel. She is educated and certified in using this type of psychotherapy, known as EMDR.

"When life, even the fun things, has a negative hold on you, it's time to see a counselor." That's what I told myself when I hit an emotional bottom in July, 2021. A negative hold meant I could no longer enjoy life or my loved ones and I could not be optimistic about anything good in the world. Shame, anger and fear ruled my life. I knew I needed help because I was not doing anything fun. I would sit in a chair lost in my own world, not wanting to do anything. Being around others was challenging because I didn't want my anger to come out at them when my fuse blew. I looked at everything negatively and found something wrong in all situations, even if something good was happening. I was just angry and would blow up at nearly every conversation. Especially those conversations held with loved ones. My wife used to say, on a scale of 0 to 10, I would go from 0 to 10 in 2.2 seconds. It was bad.

When I started looking for help years ago, I didn't believe in therapy. I learned at a young age that counselors were quacks (crazy people), and if I went to see one, I was a quack (crazy person). I feared counselors and therapy until I got a little older and couldn't stand to live with myself because I was always so angry. Additionally, I knew that spending one's life in that kind of anger was not how we should live. Not how God planned.

I decided to see a counselor when I was in my 30s, well before 2021. It was hard, but I put all the negative voices aside and made an appointment. That was the first appointment in a long journey of my work with counselors. Over the years, I have seen about 15 different ones. Typically, the need for a new counselor was because I moved locations, they decided to move on to something else, or we didn't cultivate a great relationship. Each change meant I needed to find someone new.

Once I decided upon a counselor and began to see one in person (online was not available yet), I found the routine of counseling works like the following: I talked with the counselor and it took several visits to get to know each other. Then we began to talk about some unsettling life experiences that have happened to me throughout my life that I cannot get past or process. I relived my experiences over the last 25 years with each new counselor I found, but I never found peace from my shame, anger and the rest of my emotional turmoil.

Unfortunately, I had not found successful treatment for the painful, unsettling life experiences except for medicinal. Then in November 2021, I was looking for a counselor again and after having several more that did not work out for whatever reason, I found Laurel, the counselor I have now. By searching online (which is now available) and going through a list of counselors, I scrolled until I saw a picture of Laurel. I just knew she was "the one." I felt it. After reading her bio, I knew in my gut that Laurel would make a difference in my life, and I was right. We cultivated a relationship immediately and have been solid ever since.

After several virtual online visits, Laurel asked me if I knew about EMDR, and honestly, I let her know that I had heard about it but did not know anything specific about it. From Laurel's explanation, the way I understand the process to work is when I was going through unsettling life experiences as a child, nobody taught me how to process them correctly, so I involuntarily "stuffed them" (suppressed) as far down as they would go. And then all I knew was those suppressed memories were affecting my life in ways I did not understand.

If you can, please imagine a small ball and that small ball equates to the first unsettling life experience we all seem to have… at different ages. This ball rolls and gathers all the thoughts and emotions from our second unsettling life experience, the third, fourth, etc.

By the time we are ready to work on our "sh*t," this ball is likely gigantic and tightly wound (suppressed memories). Now imagine that the ball represents our bodies. By imagining this, we can see why some of us may need counseling. This ball, our body, has become a massive cluster of emotions that cause us to feel shame, anger and fear all the time, even around things unrelated to unsettling life experiences.

The experiences in our lives that are not unsettling life experiences "stick" to the outside of the ball. I call them barnacles. They are, for instance, an argument with a loved one that escalated to something it shouldn't have but did because of how our past unsettling life experiences affected us. So, even though it was "just an argument," it was a barnacle depositing shame, anger and fear onto the side of the ball (depositing negative emotions into our minds).

EMDR helps process the unsettling life experiences and the barnacles!

Laurel and I decided to try EMDR and quickly discovered that it was helping me let go of the past and we should continue. EMDR has helped me understand how to process previous unsettling life experiences as they come back to me. I experience unbelievable freedom, peace, joy and complete happiness after they are processed. Laurel has been a blessing and true help with my achieving this freedom and peace and many other positive emotions. The ultra-exciting thing about processing these experiences is I have been able to lower the dosages of some of my medications. This psychotherapy, known as EMDR, works GREAT! So, in the following pages, I have included a couple of my experiences that show the tremendous power of EMDR.

Sadly, EMDR does not work for everyone. That fact saddens me because there is so much for one to gain from this type of therapy. While pondering this because I know it can work, maybe EMDR does not work for everyone because the counselor is not "the one" (the right fit). If you ever do not feel like you can give a counselor 100% of your trust, this will not work. Trust is the key word. If you cannot trust the counselor you are talking with, find another counselor. If that counselor isn't a good fit for you, that's not ok. You do not want to create more pain for yourself by talking to the wrong person. Find another one.

Interview until you find one that fits your

personality and the one you can trust.

There are counselors to choose from,

online and in-person, so we have many

more choices today than we did years

ago. Not all counselors are certified to do

EMDR therapy, so be sure to ask when

interviewing possible candidates.

When you finish this book, I hope you will find a great counselor, evaluate them and be ready to explore all your unsettling life experiences. Then go through this process called EMDR and afterward feel freedom and peace from the pain that has haunted you for years. Finally, I sincerely hope you will experience peace for the rest of your life.

If I can give one suggestion if you decide to do EMDR, I will say, please go into your session(s) of EMDR with an open mind, an open heart and an open soul. If you do this, I believe EMDR will work for you.

Takeaway: Once you find "the one," the right counselor, you can know you're safe, reveal all and hold nothing back

EMDR PHASES

According to (Eye Movement Desensitization and Reprocessing (EMDR) Therapy, 2017), "EMDR therapy uses a structured eight-phase approach...

Phase 1: History-taking

Phase 2: Preparing the client

Phase 3: Assessing the target memory

Phases 4-7: Processing the memory to adaptive resolution

Phase 8: Evaluating treatment results"

Each phase has requirements for Laurel and milestones for me. If I cannot get through a milestone because of the pain, we will discuss the unsettling life experience again in the next session until I reach the milestone. It may take a few minutes or several of our 50-minute sessions before I work through and complete a milestone. EMDR is hard work but so rewarding.

Who would benefit from this? Anyone with unresolved unsettling life experiences, especially people who have experienced the pain of PTSD, emotional and physical abuse, or any other abuse.

Of all the therapy I received, no one ever used EMDR, even though, according to Eye Movement Desensitization and Reprocessing (EMDR) Therapy, 2017, it was initially developed in 1987. (I began seeing the first counselor in the 1990s, but EMDR at the end of 2021). Incredibly, I had not heard of EMDR until now. I was eager to start EMDR because nothing else worked and I desperately needed help.

Takeaway: If you have unsettling life experiences from childhood or as an adult that are wrecking your life and you're tired of carrying all the baggage, look to EMDR for help. You may not have all the answers. Just bring the questions and experiences.

PHASE 1

History-Taking

It took nine weeks of therapy sessions to reach a point where Laurel and I thought I was ready for EMDR. For sanity's sake, I will include in this book what details I can of the unsettling life experiences I have been through but avoid where I must. EMDR is not easy.

History-taking happens in the first few sessions but continues throughout as Laurel and I work deeper and memories emerge. But in the first session, Laurel has questions and intake session(s) to find out more. She asks questions concerning my goals, who my partner is, and what is my support system. Laurel also asked about my parents and the relationship I had with them.

While giving the history, I must always be open and honest with Laurel. I don't mean open as in telling some things but holding others back. I mean, tell all. Open up your mind, heart and soul and bare all. I realize this might scare you, but that is not the intention. The real purpose here is to prepare you for the session(s) I hope you will have, to achieve the success possible with EMDR.

Takeaway: Honesty and openness are the only way to have successful sessions.

PHASE 2

Preparing the client

Next, Laurel explains how EMDR works. And of course, this is for the first visit only. Once I began EMDR, I knew what to expect from every session regarding how the process works.

Laurel gently lets me know what to expect regarding the possibility of a flood of emotions overtaking me due to the memories coming forward. She tells me this is ok and normal. Laurel explains that I might experience my memories in a visual form (seeing pictures from that experience) or audio form (hearing the conversation of the experience occurring but no video). My body may experience temperature changes, and I may start shaking due to nervousness or being frightened, but she lets me know that this space is safe and nobody is here to hurt me.

Laurel begins by asking me how I feel and what past unsettling life experiences are coming up for me in this session. Then, we discuss several potential candidates from those experiences mentioned and decide to focus on the one I have the most substantial negative feelings toward today.

I am feeling excited about the new treatment. I'm curious about how it will work for me, if it will work for me, and all of the intricacies that are involved. However, I am trepidatious about the possibility of facing the experiences again and wonder what memories will come up. Still, Laurel walked me gently through it and I began to relax and delve into the issue we decided to focus on for this session: the loss of a job that took place in my 20s.

The loss of this particular job was an unsettling life experience for me because of the way I lost my job. They fired me. There was no warning and there was no talking about things. This experience left me feeling shame, anger and humiliation that I could not shake. I felt bullied as an adult. These emotions I felt, coupled with all the other unsettling life experiences I've had, grew exponentially. I suffered for years due to the aftereffects of all the negative emotions stored in my body and mind.

Laurel determines if I can process the emotions that will come up around the chosen experience. Next, Laurel asks general questions about my current well-being and evaluates my body language through the virtual portal, along with my answers. Finally, she determines whether processing this memory will cause undue stress for the current session. If so, she will guide me by asking me to put the EMDR for this particular incident off for a week or until I can successfully process this one through EMDR.

I began to feel anger again toward the person I deemed as my attacker, and I felt my flight or fight response taking over a piece of me. I sense that if he was physically present at this moment, I could quickly attack him.

When Laurel and I are ready to begin EMDR, she explains that this process works by watching an animated ball go from one side of the screen to the other on my computer or another device, for example, an iPad. This watching of the ball is called bilateral stimulation (BLS). According to (What Is Bilateral Stimulation, n.d.), "Bilateral stimulation is stimuli (visual, auditory, or tactile) which occur in a rhythmic left-right pattern. For example, visual bilateral stimulation could involve watching a hand or moving light alternating from left to right and back again." The other type I have heard of is when a counselor or someone else is providing BLS and the counselor or other administrator can have the patient follow their finger(s) as they go back and forth in front of the patient's eyes.

Once Laurel brings the ball up on the screen, she explains that I am to watch the ball with my eyes only and not to move my head back and forth. Laurel then explains that she will occasionally stop the ball so we can discuss what is coming up for me regarding my thoughts and what I am seeing and feeling. Laurel will be assessing my ability to continue with EMDR at this time.

Laurel instructs me to close my eyes and imagine a container that can lock and any container will do. Still, it has to be a container that locks because it will hold the parts of the unsettling experience that we do not process and resolve in one session.

Sometimes, I talk about a life experience so involved, so detailed and unsettling that I cannot get it done in one session. At the end of my session, I consciously gathered all the pieces and parts of the experience left over, put them in my container, a vast metal garbage can and locked the lock. All the components stay locked until I unlock them in the following therapy session, which we schedule weekly. These pieces and parts can include other memories as well.

Takeaway: Relax and prepare for the emotions that will flood your mind when the memories come. What's incredible is that with your counselor's help, the emotions will not consume you.

TRIGGER WARNING: The content on these pages describes the unsettling life experiences I have had. These include child and young adult maltreatment on a physical and emotional level, without limitation. Please be watchful of this and exercise caution as necessary.

PHASE 3

Assessing the Target Memory

Laurel asks about the experience we will use EMDR on in this session. After discussing some of my other experiences, we decided the best memory today would indeed be the memories surrounding losing my job. She then asks me what I have as a negative thought about this particular experience. I tell her something like, "I am not worthy."

Laurel also asks me to think of the most positive thoughts I can have while working to resolve this particular issue. I let her know that would be, "I am awesome!" She asks what I'm feeling when I think about not being worthy and I tell her shame and anger. She then asks where I feel that shame and anger in my body. The answer can be in various physical areas, but for me, most of the time, the answer is that I feel it in my stomach, chest, shoulders, neck, or all of the above, simultaneously. Finally, she asks me to rate on a scale of 0–10 how strongly this anger feels, where 0 is no anger and 10 is the worst anger I can imagine. My first response is 20 because it's so bad. Laurel directs me to go with that memory. She reminds me to focus on that emotion and where I feel it in my body and see what comes up for me in the playback of the experience.

Laurel starts the ball going back and forth on the screen and I am anxious to see what comes up for me. Almost immediately, the memories begin flying at me. Instantly, I go back to the experience that happened, amazingly so, around 40 years ago. The memories come in the form of videos and picture snippets. I am a visual person, so it makes sense that I would get visual prompts. Others may get different prompts.

When I got my visual, I felt like I had just stepped into it. I became that young person again. Instantly, I was ready to face him and his entourage. I had real emotions, the exact ones that I had way back then, such as fear, shame and anger.

I see myself at my desk, and the branch manager (attacker) walks toward me with security guards. I'm wondering what is happening, but deep inside, I'm saying, "Uh- oh." I see my branch manager smirk, looking like his thoughts are, "I got you." That's what I feel. I also notice many of my coworkers watching as well. It's a big production. I can tell some are watching in disbelief, and others are just in shock. The branch manager and I never got along, so when he thought he had something on me that I did wrong, he exploited it and got his higher-ups to buy into the false story and they all decided to fire me. The security guards told me to pack up my things and said, "You no longer have a job." The next thing I knew, they escorted me out of the building.

I didn't know what hit me. I felt betrayed, I felt anger and shame, and I was extremely humiliated. The worst part was I considered one of the supervisors to be my friend and it seemed she would have told me about this firing ahead of time. But I had no warning at all.

The loss of my job was alarming, but not knowing it was coming and the branch manager's choice to do the actual firing in front of my peers made it seem like he meant it to be shaming.

Takeaway: There are sometimes so many thoughts and emotions that bombard us. Just know that your counselor will help walk you through which one to work on first.

PHASES 4–7

Processing the memory to adaptive resolution

Phases 4-7 are together because they are part of a direct quote, are all interwoven and can be covered better together than if I were to separate them.

Per (BehaveNet Glossaries, n.d.),

adaptive resolution is "Formerly disturbing

memories and triggers are desensitized

and more appropriate, functional

information is integrated into positive,

emotional and cognitive schema."

Periodically, Laurel stops the ball and asks me to rate the anger again from 0-10. It can get worse, stay the same or get better depending on the stage we are in, in the process. At this moment, I am still at a 10. Laurel asks me what is coming up for me. I tell her I feel everybody watching me, and I see the branch manager marching toward me with a smirk on his face. I feel very humiliated. I still have shame, fear and anger, and Laurel says, "go with that," meaning continue to think about the experience and feel those emotions.

Laurel restarts the ball going back and forth, and the videos and snippets of pictures fly at me again from behind and to the left. Finally, they fly up to my shoulder and stop. I can see everything, and I walk right back into that picture. It continues where it left off. I feel more anger as I watch the ball go back and forth, and the video progresses to him talking to me. The security guard says, "Pack up your things. You no longer have a job."

Laurel stops the ball and asks me how I'm feeling on a scale of 0–10. My answer is between 9 and 10 because the anger is still there, but something has changed. She tells me to go with that, and I start thinking about the anger I feel and what's happening to me right now as they are walking me out of the building, and I am ashamed. Over and over again, I keep thinking those thoughts. But now, the video is not progressing. The pictures are frozen. It's just me walking out with them following me or escorting me out and my coworkers watching. I just keep playing that over and over as the ball goes back and forth and back and forth. As Laurel stops the ball again, I wonder why the video froze in my mind. All I'm looking at is the same experience over and over again.

We talk about the anger and where it is on a scale of 0-10, and I tell Laurel that it's about a 5, and I'm noticing that my anger is dissipating, but I do not realize what I'm doing to make it dissipate. She asks where I feel the anger and fear and I let her know it is mainly in my chest. Then she says again, "Go with that." So, we follow the steps, breaking them down to feel them at a 4 and 3 or lower until the emotions of shame, anger, and humiliation are unbelievably gone. I am smiling and chuckling because I feel the freedom and peace I finally got after so many years from this simple process called EMDR. I take a few deep breaths and enjoy the new feelings.

Laurel asks how I am feeling and if I am ready to say the positive affirmation that I gave her at the beginning of our session. She directs me to rate on a scale of 1 to 7 how true the positive words are when I think of the experience. On this scale, 1 is I do not feel positive at all and 7 is completely positive. I say, "Yes, I'm ready! I'm at a 7!" I immediately blurt out the words that eluded me throughout the session. "I am awesome!"

By now, time is running out and it's time to wrap up. Because I was able to work through all of the emotions and memories associated with this unsettling life experience of a job loss, I did not have anything left over to lock up in my garbage can. However, if I did not get closure for this unsettling life experience, we would discuss how I would get closure by putting all the remaining memories of this disturbance into my garbage can, stuffing them in there, and locking it. That is where it was to remain until the next session. It is essential to remember those memories from other unsettling life experiences, whether critical or barnacles, can and will begin to come to the surface while working on the current experience. Those memories and any emotions present will have to be put in the garbage can, as well, until the following session.

Surprisingly enough, everything that comes up in the session that I stuff into the garbage can stays locked away for the entire time. This stuff is AMAZING!!!

Takeaway: The thoughts of unsettling life experiences bombard us negatively at first, but when worked through, we hardly spend any time on them going forward because they turn into regular thoughts.

PHASE 8

Evaluating Treatment Results

According to Posmontier, B., Dovydaitis, T., & Lipman, K. (2010), "Reevaluation occurs at the beginning of each new session to determine if treatment effects have been maintained since the last session."

At the beginning of the following week's session, Laurel started by asking me how I was doing and how my week was. I let her know I felt annoyed and frustrated for the whole week because I was getting nagged by the other previous memories of experiences that were present before we started EMDR. These memories had nothing to do with the job loss but started popping up because of the work I did for that experience.

Laurel also asks how I did with leaving everything in my garbage can, which I told her I did very well. To answer her questions, for this one unsettling experience in my life, I did not have any residual memories left over from the job loss. Still, the other experiences that were coming up I put in the garbage can to discuss at a later time. In subsequent experiences, I did very well with locking the memories in the garbage can. This simple tactic of putting the residual junk in the garbage helps in allowing me to have peace during the week between sessions. I feel free from that loss of job experience we worked through. I had a smile on my face and a skip in my step, and I felt a little like I was walking on air. I haven't felt this way in a very long time.

Once Phase 8 is done and the reevaluating of the previous EMDR session(s) for one experience is complete, phase one begins again.

Takeaway: There are relentless, unsettling life experiences we constantly think about, but when worked through EMDR, they will disappear.

PHASE 1

Next Experience

History-taking for this second experience was a little more complicated because I had only one memory. Although the job loss was a very troubling and lingering experience, it was not as unsettling as the others I eventually talked to Laurel about. One, in particular, was grounded in one sentence I had heard all my life but could not figure out why.

My father spoke of an incident related to a family trip to visit another family. My mother, the mother of the other family and my sister went somewhere to help my mom on a separate overnight visit to another city. The fathers decided that the rest of us would spend the night in tents outside. There were five of us kids and the fathers of both families.

I was seven years old then, and when it was time to get assigned sleeping quarters, I got voted to sleep with my dad in his tent. The following day, my dad said the one sentence that has stuck with me for 53 years, "Boy, you kick a lot." Even at the age of seven, I thought that was odd because I never kick in my sleep. So on the day that Laurel and I discussed it, we went through all the phases of EMDR and uncovered why the sentence stuck with me, but no other memories about this experience were present for all those years.

TRIGGER WARNING: The content on these pages describes the unsettling life experiences I have had. These include child and young adult maltreatment on a physical and emotional level, without limitation. Please be watchful of this and exercise caution as necessary.

Sometime during the night, my father raped me. Through the memories flying back to me while doing EMDR, I saw my flailing arms and legs. I saw myself trying to protect myself and stop this heinous act that was not supposed to be happening. This person, who was supposed to be my hero, shattered all trust I could ever have for him.

I believe I had suppressed it that night because, in the morning, I had no clue why he was saying that I kicked, and I had no memory of the experience until it was revealed through EMDR so many years later. I didn't even remember it, so I could tell my mom when they returned from their trip the next day. After that, the memory was gone entirely except for that one particular sentence. I felt shame and anger every day after that for 53 years, which showed in almost everything I did, but I never had a clue.

During the EMDR sessions, I cried hard and could not stop. I relived every minute of that night. The memories of the rape flew back to me the same way as the others in the job loss experience, where they flew to my shoulder from behind me and abruptly stopped.

I saw the act itself. I was trying to stop my father. I was flailing and fighting, but my little body was not strong enough to defend against him. I was crying and trying to scream during the rape but couldn't. But, I started bawling hard in the EMDR session. I couldn't stop crying either in the memory or during the session. I was so angry and full of shame.

This memory took several sessions of EMDR for me to come to a place of peace. This unsettling life experience was one for which I needed my giant metal garbage can.

Before this therapy session with Laurel ended, I had stuffed every piece of that memory into my can. Again, incredibly, storing away the memories in my garbage can allowed for freedom from those memories during the week following their stowage. EMDR allowed me to function daily, without every detail of this experience, or any other experience, being up front and the center of my attention.

Every week, EMDR revealed a little more of whichever experience we were working on at the time. Laurel and I would work on it, and then I would stow it away. The following week, I would unlock the garbage can and let out all the junk associated with this unsettling life experience and possible barnacles that were rearing their ugly heads. We would talk about what was coming up mentally for me around the experience and put the barnacles back in the can. Then, we would begin EMDR focused on the particular moment in the experience itself that was unsettling.

The 8 phases of EMDR continued in every weekly session afterward until Laurel and I worked this unsettling life experience thoroughly, and it was no longer an issue to me. Having worked my memories through EMDR, I can now process the memories that come up around my old unsettling life experiences without all the shame and anger associated with them.

Takeaway: With EMDR, you will be free of shame and anger. I would love to hear that you did it, and it worked

CONCLUSION

I hope you liked this book! While the actual experiences were hard to share, my whole purpose is to inform you, from a personal perspective, that EMDR works. When you get a counselor with whom you feel completely safe and can bare your soul, you can apply EMDR techniques to your past with their help and find a renewed quality of life. EMDR is a powerful tool.

You have reached the end of this book, but I hope it is the beginning of your journey with EMDR. I sincerely hope that my story inspired you to be a better person for yourself. There is nothing wrong with unsettling life experiences you have not worked through unless you are not facing them, and they are interfering with the quality of the life you are living today.

This book talked about the 8 phases of EMDR, how they work, and what expectations there are of you. Use the above information to find a great, SAFE counselor certified to do EMDR. Then use EMDR, now that you understand how it works, in your upcoming sessions. EMDR will help you become the best person you have ever been.

EPILOGUE

We have unsettling life experiences that
sometimes affect us from something that
may not seem awful to an outsider but
are horrific to us. Through EMDR, I have
worked through all of my unsettling life
experiences.

The most exciting thing I encountered was at the beginning of one of my sessions when I opened my garbage can to work on memories stuffed in it from the previous session. I discovered nothing was in my garbage can. NOTHING! With the help of Laurel and EMDR, I learned to process all of my unsettling life experiences.

I still work with Laurel weekly. We work on keeping me (the tightly wound ball) loose by processing the experiences that have come up for me, especially those that stuck to the outside of the ball (barnacles).

Now you have the tools. Don't let anything stop you from conquering your past. Then, you will discover freedom and peace in your future!

If you found this book helpful, I would greatly appreciate it if you left a favorable review on Amazon!

REFERENCES

BehaveNetGlossaries. (n.d.). BehaveNet.

Retrieved August 17, 2022, from

https://www.behavenet.com/adap

tive-resolution

Booth, LPC, S. (2021, March 12). EMDR Session - How Does It Really Work?: Adjust Your Perspective. Add wisdom. Create a positive learning state of mind. New Directions Counseling Services, LLC. Retrieved September 24, 2022, from https://newdirectionspgh.com/emdrsession/

Eye Movement Desensitization and

Reprocessing (EMDR) Therapy.

(2017, July 21). Clinical Practice

Guideline for the Treatment of Post

Traumatic Stress Disorder.

Retrieved August 15, 2022, from

https://www.apa.org/ptsd-

guideline/treatments/eye-

movement-reprocessing

Shapiro, F. (1989). Eye movement desensitization: A new treatment for post- traumatic stress disorder. Journal of Behavior Therapy and Experimental Psychiatry, 20(3), 211-217. https://www.sciencedirect.com/science/article/abs/pii/0005791689900256?via%3Dihub

Posmontier, B., Dovydaitis, T., & Lipman, K. (2010). Sexual violence: psychiatric healing with eye movement reprocessing and desensitization. Health care for women international, 31(8), 755–768. https://doi.org/10.1080/073993310 03725523

What is Bilateral Stimulation? (n.d.).

Anxiety Release Based on EMDR.

Retrieved August 26, 2022, from

https://anxietyreleaseapp.com/wh

at-is-bilateral-

stimulation/#:~:text=Bilateral%20

stimulation%20is%20stimuli%20(

visual,to%20right%20and%20bac

k%20again

What is EMDR? (n.d.). EMDR Institute, Inc. Retrieved August 18, 2022, from https://www.emdr.com/what-is-emdr/#:~:text=EMDR%20(Eye%20Movement%20Desensitization%20and,result%20of%20disturbing%20life%20experiences

www.ingramcontent.com/pod-product-compliance
Lightning Source LLC
Chambersburg PA
CBHW021134020426
42331CB00005B/765